In a Subjunctive Mood

David Harris

In a Subjunctive Mood

In a Subjunctive Mood
ISBN 978 1 76041 434 4
Copyright © text David Harris 2017
Cover photo – Dreamstime File ID 9778163

First published 2017 by
GINNINDERRA PRESS
PO Box 3461 Port Adelaide 5015 Australia
www.ginninderrapress.com.au

Contents

Subjunctive	7
Night flight	8
The Law	9
Butcher Bird	10
Ride the Tiger	12
Canoe Tree	13
Travelling by Camelid	14
Namatjira images	16
Hawker Creek	17
Butterfly chase	18
Golden Anniversary	19
Christmas Meccano	20
Dune Caravan	22
Christmas elbow	23
Guinness	24
Dam	26
Hell of Wool	28
The Dancers	30
Bull shoot	31
Logic	32
Shop Fever	33
The Treasurer's lament	34
Drone	35
Catalina (after Catullus)	36
Touring Terezin	38
Battle four	40
Shopping	41
Wolfie's Tale	44
Vodyánoy's Tale	47
Three Porkies	54
Catullus Poem 4	59

Subjunctive

Quizás – Perhaps.
'It takes the subjunctive,' she says.
Spanish is more careful with
the richness of its grammar.
The verb in the subjunctive mood
carries uncertainty, mystery.
explores the conditional – the imaginary.
Perhaps, perhaps,
would that it were true!
If only…
If it were possible…
Once upon a time…
Perhaps, with subjunctive –
what better way to start a story
or a poem?

Night flight

The sky tonight is cloudless,
moonless, black.
Above the haze of earth
the stars are an infinity
of brilliant jewels
sprinkled near and far.
Below me, the city is a
twinkling nebula,
a spiderweb of lights.

Tonight there's no horizon.
I'm at the centre of this sphere.
I climb up into a loop.
Venus tracks down my windscreen –
up, over,
the milky way drifts down,
passing out of sight beneath my feet.
Above my head, the city nebula appears.

Down, down, a dropping stone
towards the glittering city.
Ease back. Level out.
Back to reality.

To feel the cosmos.
To be an atom at the centre of
my own universe.

Awesome.

The Law

Watering the plants.
Hose in hand. The game –
how many can I water without moving?
I point the nozzle slowly upwards.
The stream falls further away,
its advance slowing to a stop
and with further upward tilt
begins a slow retreat.
So that's as far as I can reach from here.

Einstein visualised himself
riding on a beam of light.
I become a drop of water.
Bursting from the hose, I join my colleagues.
Together we form a glistening curve,
an elegant parabola,
all falling to earth
on the same spot.

But, in all the infinite space around us
is there no drop brave enough
to go anywhere else?
Why is this realm forbidden to us
except for this one, silver pathway?

The laws of nature – of the universe
are rigid.
They permit no deviation,
no rule-breaker, no rebel, no heretic.
There is no punishment.
Disobedience is simply impossible.

This is ultimate truth.

Butcher Bird

This actually happened while camping in the Kimberley district of WA.

He cocked his head
listening closely,
then when the echoes
of my flute's lament
across the gorge
had died away,
he began.

It was not your usual
butcher bird routine.
This was a master class.
He sang, he varied,
harmonised, vocalised,
produced an impromptu
original masterwork,
then sat back, on the top wire
of the rusty fence,
almost reachable,
awaiting my response.

I played for him an air,
beautiful, lilting,
and with his inspiration,
better than I can remember
ever playing it before.

He looked at me a moment,
then poured out a song.
Such total command.
Such effortless notes.

Obeying no man-made rules
of harmony,
he filled the air with soul.

We looked at each other,
I smiled.
I believe that he did too.
Then he flew away,
while I, in deep contentment,
rested there beside the creek.

Ride the Tiger

Illicit love springs from the tiger's lair.
If you should ride this tiger fierce and strong
you cannot then dismount, so have a care!

Love's drug is most addictive, but beware,
exhilaration carries you along –
illicit love springs from the tiger's lair

and as you ride you will become aware
that love's a carnivore, its teeth are long.
You cannot then dismount, so have a care!

Your journey may be more than you can bear,
eternal vigilance must be lifelong.
Illicit love springs from the tiger's lair,

for should you fall, then those whose lives you share
will suffer too with you, you do them wrong.
You cannot then dismount, so have a care!

The tiger may be tamed, but be aware –
a wild beast it remains. It's fierce, headstrong.
Illicit love springs from the tiger's lair.

So spring onto the tiger if you dare;
and give your soul to love's impassioned song!
Illicit love springs from the tiger's lair –
You cannot then dismount, so have a care!

Canoe Tree

Cars rush past along the Goolwa road;
Ngarrendjerri country this. The bush,
the creeks, the lakes, the fish, the birds,
the old, old trees. Casuarina,
stringybark, majestic river reds.
And now the road.

There is a red gum by this road.
Canoe tree. The huge scar on its side
is turned away – ashamed?
Or best to hide from sightless eyes
its story and its place in this, its land.

A hundred years ago this tree was young.
Tall, upright, smooth of bark, crowned with leaves.
A man came by. His need, a bark canoe,
to hunt for fish. With axe of stone he cut
and pried away the smoothest of the bark.

At first, the raw, torn wood formed scars which,
over time, turned smooth, round-edged, discreet.
Its life began anew that day. What happened
to the man we do not know. Perhaps
his spirit lives in song and dance.
No doubt his bark canoe survived a few brief years.
The tree lived on, and lives with us today.

The tenuous shoots that showed above the scar
in that first spring, are now the boughs,
as large as trees themselves, with limbs and leaves.
Canoe tree. Its shape encapsulates its life.

Travelling by Camelid

'The camel has a single hump;
the dromedary, two –
or p'rhaps the other way around –
I'm never sure! Are you?'

The poet Ogden Nash, not I
set out this little verse,
and now I'm sure I'll never know –
he's made it that much worse!

Some say a camel is a horse
produced by a committee.
I feel that that's a bit unkind,
it's really such a pity.

The horse is swift and strong and proud;
the camel slow and graceful.
The dromedary's graceful, too –
both feel that haste's distasteful.

The camel and the dromed'ry
embody in their style
some features of my current life
I've noticed for a while;

I've gathered quite a strong dislike
for speed and for aggression.
Where once life's rapids stirred my blood,
today, a slow progression

gives pleasure to the journey and
builds up anticipation,
a sort of antipasto which
adds much to consummation.

I'm happy, too, to go along
unsure of things at times;
a camel or a dromed'ry?
You're only playing games.

So push your red Ferrari
with its mighty, throaty roar.
It stirs up your adrenalin
but I just say 'what for?'

I've sped around that racetrack now
quite often in my life.
Arriving at the goal, I've found
is rarely worth the strife.

So now, I gently glide through life
sedately in my Prius,
I'm travelling camel slowly so
that everyone can see us.

Namatjira images

Ghost gums, scattered trees, bare hills, open plains.
Memories flood in
from the storehouse of experience
to add what the painting cannot show.

A cooling breeze relieves the heat.
Boots crunch on the rocky path.
A swig of cold water tastes of nectar.

Drawn ever deeper by the artist's skill
into scent, that most evocative of senses.
Smell the bush, aromatic, spicy, dusty.

Deeper still, now feel the spirit,
timeless harmony of ancient people,
ancient land. This is country.

Hawker Creek

Long walk to get here.
Quiet. Hot.
Just bush sounds,
a rustle, a distant crow.

The slab of pink marble
from the gorge wall
fell across the creek.
Shattered into pieces
millennia ago.

Water bubbles now
between smooth boulders,
flowing deep, green,
through pink crevasses.

Old as the hills –
600 million years.
Water flows, gurgles, splashes.
The creek is alive,
refreshes me,
as it has always done for visitors,
from dinosaurs to people.

So I am here.
The blink of an eye
in this land's time.
And yet the creek
puts its loving care
into the task of
cooling my feet.

Butterfly chase

From my vantage point on the ladder
they are at eye level.
The butterfly, flying for its life,
a wagtail in hot pursuit.

It seems no contest.
The bird, so quick, so agile
and yet each time it darts in –
a split-second manoeuvre –
too fast for eye to follow,
and the butterfly escapes.

The bird attacks again.
Result the same.
Then they disappear
behind the shed.

Golden Anniversary

Just fifty years ago today you wed
the man you loved. You grew in love each day
as life together, children, work and play,
like waves upon the rocks, reshaped you both.
Rough corners rubbed away, re-formed,
you meshed more closely to each other.
Decades passed.

In love's maturity, you and he became
the two the world then came to know as one.
Life brought its share of tests; you both emerged
the stronger. Confident, you looked ahead
to share a twilight peace together.

Bur it was not to be. You wrote with love
of those last months together, and your loss.
The woman you are now was formed with him,
and after him as grief laid down its scars.
These scars are softening now. Your life goes on,
as gentle metamorphosis takes place.

And now you are with me. We share a love
as strong as any I have known. And yet…
At moments like today I see you pass
as through some magic door, unknown to me
where once again together, you and he
are back, familiar, intimate again.

Christmas Meccano

My Christmas presents always fell
in one of three divisions –
Useless: clothes aren't presents!
Acceptable: books, perhaps, if
documentary or adventure.
But there was one, and only one,
I put on Santa's list (and got) each year –
Meccano!

I don't recall my very first Meccano set.
It must have been quite small,
but taught me basic stuff, like how
to tighten nuts (that's clockwise, son)
and how to fit the parts together.
I quickly learned to read the manuals.
Useful stuff, not fairy stories!
Until, when I was eight or nine,
there wasn't much within the books
I couldn't make – on Christmas Day.

My Grandpa died when I was nine,
and in the clearing of his house
my Dad unearthed a treasure trove –
Meccano sets he had received.
With feelings only Dad and I
could really understand, we took
the precious parts out of their box.
Their quality was quite superb,
and colours, too, were different.

I made a few more models, but
the gift of old Meccano also marked
a turning point in life, the end
of youngest childhood and the start
of a more serious phase.
The loss of Grandpa, and the gift
that I saw as his last to me;
more serious school,
we moved house too.
Life now took on a different path,
and I was growing up.

Dune Caravan

The sculptured shapes
of wind-formed desert dunes
attract the artist.
Clean lines against the hard blue sky.

Your skin, the colour of pale desert sand,
your shoulders satin-smooth,
form such a landscape, where my eyes
pass as a caravan.

You read, I hold you close,
my arm across your body.
At end of day, your scent is softened
from its hours upon your skin.

Across the dunes a tiny stream runs by –
your silver neck-chain.
Here a glitter, there a lazy loop becomes
a quiet billabong.

This desert traveller, in among the dunes
enjoys the scene.

Christmas elbow

While some watched tennis tournaments at Christmas
with serves and volleys, temperament and heat,
we had some other drama, fuelled by Bacchus –
exchanges that could be quite indiscreet.

With background yells from noisy, raucous kids,
contestants faced each other, glare for glare.
Anne opened with a sizzling serve, at Mildred
'Your children are disgraceful! Don't you care?'

The volley back from Mildred was a beauty –
a pity that they called it: 'out of bounds'.
The words included 'broomstick' – also 'Nazi'
and others had to do with female hounds.

It went from bad to worse with temper tantrums
we're lucky that it didn't come to blows.
I thought that they would tear themselves apart.
It was a day of drama, heaven knows.

So late that night, long after the crescendo,
with scotch in hand, reliving blow by blow,
I found that I had got a tennis elbow
from lifting out the turkey from the stove!

Guinness

A glass of Guinness holds a magic.
Freshly drawn, opaque with foam,
it grips, enthralled, the dark stout tragic.
It's as soulful as a poem.

It's not about anticipation
of another night of sin,
more to do with contemplation
of the wond'rous sight within.

For this quencher of a thirst
contains a magic, filled with awe
(observed at best not in the first
but after two, or three, or more).

On the top a head is forming,
then you'll notice something queer,
underneath the frothy storming
you will see the liquid clear,

Though the lower part is clearing
and the head forms on the crown,
all the bubbles are not rising
all, it seems, are falling down!

If you wait a little longer
(standing up or lying down)
you will have a glass of stronger
liquid, clear up to its crown.

If this wondrous observation
brings a philosophic mood,
you will note a clear relation –
life, and love, and human good.

Life is like a fresh-poured Guinness,
murky, roiling darkest beer.
When all around, it seems, is falling
wait, and it will all come clear.

If life's meaning you will ponder
and as well, you like a drink,
Guinness brings the two together.
Deep imbibe and deeply think.

Dam

Under laboratory Health and Safety,
surely important though it is
dealing with topics obscure and weighty,
things that go 'bang' and others that fizz,
grows a bureaucracy, most bureaucratic,
lots of rules saying 'thou shalt not'
and detailed instructions, so dogmatic,
we must obey to the very last dot.

So when we were told 'all spills must be dammed,
using the sand which is provided,
safety provisions have all been planned'
we scanned the documents, double-sided –
only to find we had been mistaken,
now that we had the instructions in hand,
we could read, and were really quite shaken,
that all of our spills must now be DAMNED!

What is the point of the sand, we demand?
Better some training in spells and curses!
For if our spills are indeed to be damned
all of us must take appropriate courses.
To practise, I made a small spill on the bench,
addressed it with face of accusatory ire –
'Damn you, foul spill' through teeth all a-clench
I mouthed, but the spill didn't move, or retire.

We searched for appropriate courses thematic,
for damning a spill, off to Hell for its sins,
but while we found Tarot, Astrology, Magic,
courses on sex and baroque violins,
on witchcraft and wandcraft we found not a sign.
We needed a wand. Suzie brought in a chopstick.
It did look the part but it turned out benign –
and waving it round made us feel idiotic.

So, back to the source of this document strange,
we need explanation on just what to do.
We mentioned in passing our need to arrange
appropriate training in spells and voodoo.
The looks we received made us quake in our boots,
we pointed in vain to the document text
which clearly said 'damning'. 'I don't care two hoots!
I don't give a dam about spelling! What next!'

'You know what's intended, you ignorant twits!
Let all spelling Nazis move over to arts!
We're engineers here, we're not pickers of nits,
just trying to help you, you ignorant farts!'
So now, should we ever a foul liquid spill
we build up a dam using sand from our bucket
and then, with a muster of greatest goodwill
we curse the thing, softly, and don't just say…

    any words which may give offence to some people.

Hell of Wool

Warm day, dappled sunlight,
wine with lunch,
comfortable chair.
Writers' festival drones on.

I want to listen to the author
speaking of her book,
but concentration fades,
thoughts drift,
eyelids droop,
reality recedes.

She is from New Zealand.
Her words cavort
in my mind, distorted by
her strong accent.
Was that child *tin yeeres* old?
Was she really going to *shear* her story?
Remove woolly edges, perhaps?

Her book title I heard as
'A Hell of W'll'. Wool?

My Aunt Rachel used to knit jumpers
that were a hell of wool
She had a reputation as
a tight knitter.
Her jumpers had a texture
between felt and leather.
Very frugal, she'd collect,
unpick and reuse old jumpers.

Misshapen, odd colours –
fashion items they were not.
Great fishing jumpers.
Windproof, spray-proof,
stained with fish blood,
the odd scale adhering.
I can smell the boat!

I shake my head, force eyes open.
How did I get down this path?
Focus…

Oh, to *hill* with it!
Eyelids, shut out the world.
Let doze descend.

The Dancers

Around, around the Jewish dancers whirl,
blonde, blue-eyed girls all dressed in modest grey,
their hair, that sinful turner of men's heads,
appropriately hidden from all view.

Here in the ancient synagogue we sit.
Today, the women sit amongst the men.
Three quarters of a century have passed
since Torah last was read within its walls.

The town of Třebíč has two synagogues,
the newer, on the tourist trail, and then
the ghetto, now called 'Jewish Town' and in
its cemetery there lie ten thousand souls.

Its Jewish history, evident throughout
and recognised as Europe's heritage,
sits oddly with the fact that in this town
no Jews have lived since 1944.

Around, around the Jewish dancers whirl,
although, of course, these dancers are not Jews.
I feel discomfort. In their innocence
they dance on many centuries of graves.

Bull shoot

While touring in Spain…

The bulls are everywhere.
Not common, but each few hours
a hillside, and there, the huge bull,
a silhouette, proud, muscled, iconic.
We need a photograph.
To shoot the bull, from
on the highway, at 120 clicks –
less than 15 seconds.
See a bull,
    remember that you want a photo,
        dig for camera in travel bag,
            remove from camera case,
                take off sunnies
                      find specs and put on,
                            check camera settings,

point at bull –
damn, it's gone!
Keep camera at the ready, and
no bull will appear.
Putting away the camera
makes a bull appear.
Many bulls we've seen.
Just a few photos,
mostly side on, behind trees.
We can always buy postcards.

Logic

IF... THEN... ELSE
IF (true)
THEN (do this, or)
ELSE (do that).
Boolean Logic.
Clear, precise,
no shades of grey.

so...IF that is true –
I only have your word for it.
I trust you, but your black and white
has grey edges. Maybe.
But IF it is, as you say, true
THEN I – we – must do this?
You agree?

So in my chart of life
where shall I place the pin?
Firmly in the black –
my IF test yielding 'TRUE',
or perhaps at some point
in the fringe of grey.
'TRUE-ish?'

That little question mark –
it is my ELSE.
Is it written faint or bold?
How much must I look
into your eyes,
or read between the lines
a possible Plan B?

Shop Fever

With apologies to John Masefield's 'Sea Fever'

I must go down to the shops again,
to the lovely shops in the mall,
and all I ask is a credit card
and an ATM on the wall,
and the bustling crowds and the winter sales
and the spruikers crying,
and some clothes I love at a discount price,
and the buying, buying, buying.

I must go down to the shops again,
for the call of consumer pride
is a loud call, and a clear call
that cannot be denied,
and all I ask is a faithful friend
with a focus on consuming,
whose joy in life is to spend and spend
on glamour and on grooming.

I must go down to the shops again,
to the self-indulgent life,
for it's my way, it's the girl's way,
my escape from the daily strife.
And all I ask is a cappuccino
and a passionfruit pavlova,
with a lovely chat in the coffee shop
when the long shop's over.

The Treasurer's lament

The Treasurer's lot is a lonely one
far away from the life poetic.
While others are having lots of fun
with cups of tea and an Easter bun
the Treasurer's work is never done
and it's dull as an anaesthetic.

'Have you paid your subs?' like a record stuck,
but it falls on ears unhearing.
You haven't paid, well, you're out of luck,
you're not in my book, off the list you are struck,
when it comes down to money, you don't give a damn
and for me you are uncaring.

Nobody loves the hard-working Treasurer
There's nothing poetic about the role
Look at the words that rhyme – tax gatherer,
usurer, labourer, fritterer, murderer.
Tell me, pray, what could be absurderer?
Spreadsheets be damned, I'm reclaiming my soul!

Drone

So tell me, colonel, once again, just how you know
your target, a mere pixel image on a screen,
deserved your Hellfire missile with its hammer blow.

You say your mission violates no law, and so –
oh yes, you said no *law of war* that you have seen.
So tell me, colonel, once again, just how you know.

Your men had brought in an informer of the 'foe'
who told you that a village house where he had been
deserved your Hellfire missile with its hammer blow.

Oh, by the way, the party in the house laid low
was a betrothal, for new lives that might have been…
So tell me, colonel, once again, just how you know.

The groom-to-be was Taliban, he had to go!
That youth, excited, swept along, and just eighteen –
deserved your Hellfire missile with its hammer blow?

I've heard that your informant left some time ago
to tend his poppy crop – it won't make just morphine!
So tell me, colonel, once again, just how you know –
they all deserved your missile with its hammer blow?

Catalina (after Catullus)

Inspired by the style and imagery of Catullus 'Poem 4', reproduced on page 59

The plane you see there, friends, now high and dry,
no longer flies. Restored
by loving, understanding hands to what it was, they've left
the bullet holes, repairs and dents,
and yet, is it not strange
how battle scars degrade it not at all,
and such a weapon still remains a thing of grace?

A child, I saw it first moored off the river shore,
the ocean bird, at home among the clouds, at rest
by night, a moonbeam ladder on the waves
reached to her hull, slap slopping in the still,
warm air of starry summer night.
My uncle was its pilot.
That night we were at war.

Next morning, with her weapon load renewed,
her tanks refilled, her crew of half a dozen men,
so brave, so young would once again
take to the sky, to hunt and to be hunted
far above the lovely, island spangled
ocean to the north, or skim across the waves
in darkest night to lay its dragon eggs
amongst their navy's ships.

The Catalina, high in tropic sky,
scourge of the submariner,
the eyes, and, too, the fangs of our defence
patrolled the air above the Timor sea,
the Torres and Malacca Straits
beneath the threatening shadow of Imperial Japan.
But now she rests, not as so many of her kind
in ocean depths, inhabited by spirit crews,
my uncle and his friends.
She now grows old with grace.
In dedication to the shrinking band of ageing men
who flew in her, I, who was that child, salute you.

Touring Terezin

The overwhelming sense is one
of sheer efficiency. The map
of Poland shows them clearly marked
as squares, the death camps – Auschwitz,
Chelmno, Sobibor, Treblinka, Majaduch
where prisoners' lives were measured in
a few brief hours. Where ovens burned
unceasingly, through day and night.

A circle shows each concentration camp,
including where I stand in Terezin.
Again, the map is clear – how it
supplied a steady flow of victims, to ensure
efficient rates of killing were maintained.

A scattering of smaller circles shows
the ghettos in the towns, the local camps,
there must have been a hundred on this map,
which served, within this vast machine,
as concentrating feeders to the camps.

But, looking at the map, the thought arose,
'I wonder who designed this thing?
Did they call in consultants for
its project management? Who engineered
the ovens, with such huge capacity?
How did rail freight operators calculate
how many cattle trucks they needed in a train?'

And overall, the system met its goals.
Today there are not many Jews in Europe.
This single wall map, showing as it does
the layout of a functional, efficient,
and effective genocide machine –
of which designers could be rightly proud –
makes trembling chills go running up my spine.

The Czech town of Terezin is also often known by its German name, Theresienstadt.

Battle four

We taxi out,
four young men,
four silver jets.
Unlikely warriors.

Two by two we speed,
runway lights a blur,
ground drops away,
up into the cloud.

In tight formation
four misty shapes,
so close the faces
of my friends are clear.

Suddenly – free.
Burst from the cloud top,
white in sunlight,
four silver darts streak
into an azure sky.

Our guns are armed.
Our birds are weapons.
We are killing machines.
Bur in our youth and innocence
the joy of flight is orgasmic.

Shopping

This tale lies on the boundary between poetry and prose. It is written as a short story, but entirely in iambic, poetic rhythm.

I know it was a weapon-selling fair, an international expo of defence, and I was there as part of it, and yet I did not fit. My academic work would help to train, to analyse, to understand, to plan. Two centuries ago the great von Clausewitz declared that 'War is the continuation of *die Politik* by other means.' My work was closer to the *politik*, but here, today the 'other means' were what was on display.

The customers were men in suits, or men in uniform, of blue, khaki or white, all dripping gold from epaulette and collar, cap and sleeve, out on a shopping spree in this great expo of the latest, best and sexiest of these, the ultimate in toys for boys. And in the air there hung a tangible miasma of testosterone, aggression and machismo. Primal. Dark.

There were some women in amongst the crowd. A few in business black or uniform. A very few. But there were many more within the cubicles or on the stands displaying all the offerings of war. They were, of course, all expert in their field, as were their colleagues in their business suits. Oh yes, the men were always there – I did not see a stand with women and no men. But expert though they were, their role was clear – they were the magnet, the eye candy, to attract the suckers in.

When women are employed to fill this role, it's clear they are selected and prepared with care and skill to press the buttons of their targets – sorry, 'clients'. And their age range is important – 30-plus, on into 40s, not beyond. Not model-thin, not overweight – it seems at times that they have had to pass through some imagined gauge, a 'go' and 'not go' template for their shape. Intelligent, well-spoken, full of charm. Their dress conservative – and yet… I watched as women from this rigid mould collected little crowds of smiling men to sell them new torpedoes, guns and bombs, discussed the cannon shells they had displayed, their bunker-buster weapons, their grenades. I watched the charming woman spruiking Bofors, watched the video with which she showed the increased killing radius of anti-aircraft shells and how effective they could also be on 'personnel'.

In this surreal atmosphere I saw these men as nothing more than law-supported bikies. Tribal, macho, careless of the rights of other men whose crime is to support a different tribe. Today the bikies have declared a truce, allowing them to come together in this hall, to see new weaponry, to learn new skills, to forge new contacts. So today Hell's Angel brushes shoulders with a Rebel, here Chinese and Russian gather round, share coffee and converse.

We cannot stretch the metaphor too far. The bikie's woman – 'bitch' defines her role as loyalty, availability and, over all, submission. If the women selling weapons are aloof from this, how well they know that, with a little stroking of an ego, with a hint of sexiness and caring, then a sale is easier made.

For me, the take-home message came as I was thinking it was time to leave. A little knot of soldiers gathered closely round a woman from the mould. In ivory suit with turquoise satin top, her three-inch heels were elegant, not tarty. Her blonde hair shoulder-length (bikie mantra 'long hair's better – always!'), she was standing close beside their leader, he with grin from ear to ear. I caught the faintest whiff – was it Chanel? – as she held firmly to his shoulder a sample of her company's product – a deadly sniper rifle.

Far from the heat of battle, from the passion and the roar, the sniper plies his trade, selecting, aiming, killing. His rifle is the weapon of a murderer. I left.

Wolfie's Tale

The Mongolians hold that powdered wolf's rectum is an effective treatment for haemorrhoids. There are several possible ways to interpret this...

Astride a sturdy Mongol horse
the wolf hunt, with Mongolian bow,
the age-old sport of Mongol kings
is what the ancient paintings show.

And yet there is another hunt
the wolf, as best he can, avoids,
for powdered rectum of the wolf,
they say will clear up haemorrhoids.

The shaman, mystic magic man,
provides the powder for the task –
what's added to his talcum tins
the people are afraid to ask.

They know they must not harm the wolf;
instructions, though, were quite unclear
on how to wring the magic cure
out from the wolf's, when powdered, rear.

There was a tribal chieftain who,
in depths of suffering from piles,
one morn dispatched a wolf-hunt band
to catch one – let them ride for miles.

He followed on, his saddle deep
with feather down and cotton padded,
while he, and others, ruminated
how powdered rear, to his, be added.

At last a wolf they came upon,
lassoed him fast, and tied him down.
They raised his tail, and thickly powdered
all that, there, was coloured brown.

How their chieftain's piles they treated
none of them would let be known.
So you, dear reader, if you wish
can speculate it on your own.

We should feel sorry for the wolf.
He howled, and galloped off in shame;
he never could rejoin his pack,
and never knew who was to blame.

And now, where'er he sits, he leaves
white patches on the barren ground
and late at night his mournful howl
is such a deep, heart-wrenching sound.

The old wives' tale which launched this hunt
was based upon some truth indeed,
but this had now become deranged
by human arrogance and greed.

A special powder, if applied to
Wolfie's stern is efficacious,
but only for his haemorrhoids
and not for human ones! Good gracious.

Vodyánoy's Tale

Part 1

'Thank you, fellow Vampires, for your presence.
You all are warmly welcome in this place.'
Rusálka's* voice, as rich as Porto wine
– which even now was warming hearts and minds –
went on, 'And now, Vodyánoy, if you will,
the Incantation.' I arose, I met
their eyes, and then began 'Oh spirits dead…'
and as the words, familiar, full of awe
reverberated round the cavern walls,
the spirits of the past were here, with us.
Our meeting had begun. Rusálka called
on Brendan to report.

Bishop Brendan Flaherty DD
– our Vampire colleague – has a human name,
and form more softened, rounded, aged, to suit
his long and fruitful placement as our man
inside the Vatican. The Vampire world
must know its foes – what better way than to
embed ourselves inside their citadels.
And so it is this evening that we meet
to study Brendan's new report, prepared
at noble lord Rusálka's own command.

He stood, head bowed, in meditation deep;
we waited for his words.

---

* Vodyánoy and Rusálka are genuine Vampire names. Brendan's Vampire name is Dovonoi, but for security reasons, his human name is used within the Vampire world.

Part 2

They stand expectantly: how can they know?
Achieving bishop rank, the move to Rome
requires apprenticeship and years of work –
but not for me! The human Bishop was
my victim. I absorbed his blood, his life,
his name, persona, knowledge and his shape –
his friends and colleagues took me to be him.
In those first decades of my term, the church,
the Curia in Rome, were closing ranks
against an ever-growing cloud of evil deeds
through which nocturnal sanguinary needs
were never seen. My life was quite secure.

Secure as well beneath my Vampire cloak,
from the skins of ancient Vampire martyrs slain,
protecting me from crosses, prayers and from
the Christian forces ever-present here
in this so turgid atmosphere of 'good'!

And then the Earth moved underneath my feet
not once, but twice my stable world was rocked.

The first – Rusálka's stunning brief to me:
'Does transubstantiation make wine blood?'

One morning, in Communion's daily rite
I went without my cloak – but then I felt
the spirit penetrate into my heart.
It was as scales fell from before my eyes.

The second followed from the first, in James.
The mentor I discovered as my guide.
A man so good, so pure and yet so strong,
I fell in love with him – in Vampire love –
I lusted for his life force, for his blood.

He knew this, he had seen the void within
where soul should be. He gladly gave his life
to me. We are now one. I love his God.
Now I must speak.

Part 3

'My colleagues, I was humbled to receive
your brief, instructing me to bring to you
a full report, of doctrine, evidence
and fact on Transubstantiation.

My friends – this was a task!'

He paused, seemed to collect his thoughts:
'Here is not time or place to talk about
our fear and deep distrust of Christian faith.
We have our martyrs. Yet within that faith
we find a common thread with Vampire kind.

We often ridicule their sacrament –
a little bread and wine, a mere pretence
of our consumption of live flesh and blood!
And yet, they feel a full communion with
their "Christ" as deep as any that we draw
out from our victims. In this sacrament
is clearly more at work than bread and wine.

The statement of their Christ "This is my blood…"
when passing on to all a cup of wine
is central to Communion, this, their rite
wherein a cup of wine is blessed, and then becomes
transformed into the holy blood of Christ.'

Part 4

It was as if his words had killed all sound.
A silence filled the cave, then in its turn
was shattered – shards of darkness flying out
as startled bats into the night. The Lord
Rusálka's angry voice rang out. 'What! What!
Transformed, you say? Transformed to living blood?'

'That is the "Transubstantiation"
you asked me to report upon, and yet
the deeper did I delve into the word,
the deeper did its mystery become.'
Brendan's voice fell silent. Then went on,
'I am a bishop of the Church of Rome.
Each working day begins with prayer and with
a Mass, at which all present take – Communion.
For thirty years, my days as bishop and
my nights as Vampire satisfied me well,
but recently, to meet your brief I have
allowed the spirit of the sacrament
to penetrate me, as it does my colleagues.
This spirit is the transformation key.'
'Your words, dear Brendan, give me grief and pain.'
Rusálka's voice was trembling from his lips.

'This Transubstantiation you have seen,
does it have use or even relevance
to us? And is it myth or is it truth?'

'Ah, noble Lord, that question "What is truth?"
Does wine turn into blood? In Christendom
some say it does, some others not.
Some call it parable, some call it fact.
And yet all Christians hold it to be true
that Christ is present with them as they drink.'
'That is no answer! Tell us more!'
     'My Lord
you love good music. Transported, you will
hear it speak to you, its meaning clear,
but well you know that meaning cannot be
expressed in words. As music is much more
than simple sounds, so is the full gestalt
of Transubstantiation more than bread
and wine. It does not happen in the place
of worldly things, but at their meeting point
with mind and spirit.'

Rusálka spoke: 'Good Brendan, we have heard
you out, reporting on the facts, so very clear,
that Transubstantiation must occur
in places highly toxic to our kind.
Your strength and dedication we respect,
your knowledge and your wisdom sorely need.
Return to Rome. Your task today is done.'

Part 5

We sat in silence, just the two of us,
Rusálka and I, who also have his trust.
Cold sadness and despair hung in the air.
We know what must be done, must be done now.
'So Brendan must now die!' Rusálka's teeth
clenched tight, resisting every word that passed.
'We all have judged. Now you, Vodyánoy, must
be executioner. Go quickly now and do
with grace and dignity, your awful task.'

Part 6

I fly so swiftly on throughout the night,
my mind a churning mass of thoughts, of doubts
and fear. I see the dreadful fate which has
befallen Brendan. He has devoured
a life so good, so strong that it has filled
his body with a soul, which brings with it
his death. He is no longer Vampire kind.
Why could this not have been foreseen? Dispatched
to live within the heart of Christian power.
To live as Christian – as a priest indeed,
his Vampire self suppressed, exposed each day
to feared discovery and death.
Maintaining this deception takes its toll.
Researching deeply into their beliefs
could only weaken his defensive shield.
Today, and at my hand, he now must die.

His crime – to do his best to undertake
a task of awful risk – and then to fall.
I fly so swiftly on throughout the night.
God only knows what our tomorrow brings.

Three Porkies

'The Three Little Pigs' revisited

Daily Flash, 16 July
White Shoe Brigade alive and well!
Despite warnings from authorities, it seems that people are still falling for 'too good to be true' rorts by shady property developers. Full report page 20…

They say a fool and money are soon parted.
The more the cash, the easier the parting.
That's my experience. It's been the guiding light
behind Lupo Developments since our first day.
So when the Bacon sisters won the lotto prize
I smelled the kind of meat old Wolfie loves.
I had a new development to sell.
Green fields, prime riverside, great views.
Much later I was told it was flood plain. But then,
I feel there are some things it's better not
to know. So I tend often not to ask.

Daily Flash, 15 January
'House of straw' claim.
Families who bought new houses from a well-known local property developer now claim shoddy workmanship and flooding. Full report page 14…

They bought the house I offered off the plan.
Three bedrooms, one for each, and lots of glass
to catch the river views. Paid up the full
deposit, and we got to work. It had
to be completed pretty quick – before
the wet arrived. It was. They paid in cash.

The rain this season wasn't really bad.
Perhaps a bit above the norm, but then
it only came an inch above the floors.
Panic! The phone exploded in my ear
and though I tried to stall, they wouldn't have
a bar of it. 'Come here at once!' I came.
That day the rain peed down. The creeks that crossed the road
were running deep, when through the mist ahead
a four-wheel drive appeared, then passed – the Bacon girls!
They'd had enough. I pressed on cautiously, and soon
arrived at Bacons' house – or what was left of it!
It had half fallen down, and as I watched, another wall
crashed down to join the growing wreckage pile.
The road was clear – we'd built it up a bit. When through
the mist, a ragged group of suckers – sorry, clients –
came marching towards me. I didn't wait. A quick
U-turn and I was off. They stayed and watched the slow
collapse. They blamed it all on me. Perhaps that's where
that silly tale of Wolfie's huff and puff took off.
I reckon that I knew what had gone wrong.
This is a cut-throat business, your profit
comes mainly from the things you can leave out
without the owner noticing. But with
the Bacons – no such luck. They came on site
most days, insisted that we build to spec.
About the only place I saved some cash
was in foundations. We had a bit of
old cement – not much, and pretty stale.

The reinforcement we removed one night
to use on yet another job. So I suppose
the Bacons' place was really built on sand.

Daily Flash, 13 September
'House of sticks' claim.
New 'luxury timber dwellings' built by troubled property developer now flagged as fire hazards. Poor quality electrical work blamed for several fires. Special report page 4…

With lawyers and departments on my tail
it took some real fast talking on my part
to stop investigation, and the really
nasty things that that it could bring in train.
I had to promise to rebuild the house,
flood-proof (more cost in drains!). And it was done.
It cost a shitload, best of timber, best
of everything, but with inspectors there,
dropping by on every other day,
I had no choice. There was one tiny saving
that I made. The electrician's quote
was off the planet! I knew my mate Nguyen
had got a crew of boat people – real cheap!
So wiring up was done at half the cost.
Next time the Bacons called me to the house
the background when they passed me wasn't mist
but smoke. To lose the house was bad enough
but when it set the bush on fire, the shit
then really hit the fan. A lawyers' feast.

Daily Flash, 12 December
'House of bricks' outcome.
Victims of shoddy workmanship house fire awarded major damages. Builder forced to provide complete new house. Continued on page 18...

This time they got a lawyer
that skinny, thin-lipped smart-arse, Lottie Hamm.
They say Hamm starts her day by sucking
on a lemon, washed down with half a cup
of blood – it should be male. They froze my
assets, took me off to court, then skinned me clean.
They had my parts caught firmly in a vice
and tightened up the screws until I wept.
Next time they got an effin' mansion.
Solid brick, two-storey. On a different
block – and higher. They really roasted me.

Daily Flash, 29 January
Shonky developer shows up in NT.
Government money intended for worthy cause ends up in hands of developer with shady track record. In-depth report page 20...

Lost the house. Lost the Merc. Lost the girlfriend.
But now, you know, I've found that when you start
from nothing, there really isn't any more to lose.
Started with a name change. Lupo is now Wolfgang
(get it?) – the surname Schwindler matches. Good solid
German – hard-working, trustworthy. Helpful image.

I'm based in Katherine now, the business name's
Indigenous Housing Inc. You know, in this you
just can't lose. All public money. No one queries
what you charge. The clients, too, are hardly in position
to complain of quality. It's only been
a coupla months, but now I'm doing well.
The money flows like through a fire hose here
into the bank. I'll be set up for life.
Give me a few years yet, and I'll be back
enjoying Gold Coast life, just like old times.

Catullus Poem 4

That yacht, which you see, my guests
says that it was the fastest of ships
and that it was able to see off
the challenge of any floating ship
whether with small oars or sail.
There would be a need for it to fly
and my yacht denies that the shore
of the menacing Adriatic denies this –
or the Cycladic islands or
well-known Rhodes and the choppy Thracians –
Propontis or the cruel Pontic sea.

Where that this later yacht before was
a leafy forest; for on a ridge of Mt Cytorus,
with its chattering leaves often it
gave out a whistling sound.
O Pontic Amastris and box tree bearing Cytorus,
to you these things have been,
and still are, very well known.
My yacht says, from its earliest beginning
it says that it has stood on your peak
it has dipped its little oars in your water
and then through so many raging seas
it carried its master, whether a left or a right breeze
would call, or a favourable wind
from Jupiter had fallen
on both sheets at the same time.

Nor had any vows to the gods of the shore
been made by it when it was coming
from the last sea up to this clear lake.
But these things were earlier: now with its
secluded rest it grows old and dedicates itself to you,
O twin Castor and Twin of Castor.

www.ingramcontent.com/pod-product-compliance
Lightning Source LLC
Chambersburg PA
CBHW062202100526
44589CB00014B/1921